Roman Government!
Ancient History for Kids
From the Emperor to the Senate
Children's Ancient History Books

Left Brain Kids
Educational Books for Children

There were three types of governments in Ancient Roman times, and these were: Monarchy, Republic and Empire.

In its earlier period, Rome was under a monarchy. It was ruled by a man named Romulus.

In 509 B.C., the ancient people of Rome gained control and established the Roman Republic.

In the Roman Republic, the people owned the country and were no longer ruled by a single person.

The highest position in the Republic was called the Consul.

Every year, two Consuls ruled at the same time. This kept any one Consul from becoming too powerful.

The people elected officials, including Consuls and Senators, to serve for a limited period of time.

Soon after, Rome's senators started to fight and they began to become violent towards one another. Because of this, the Roman Republic began to fall.

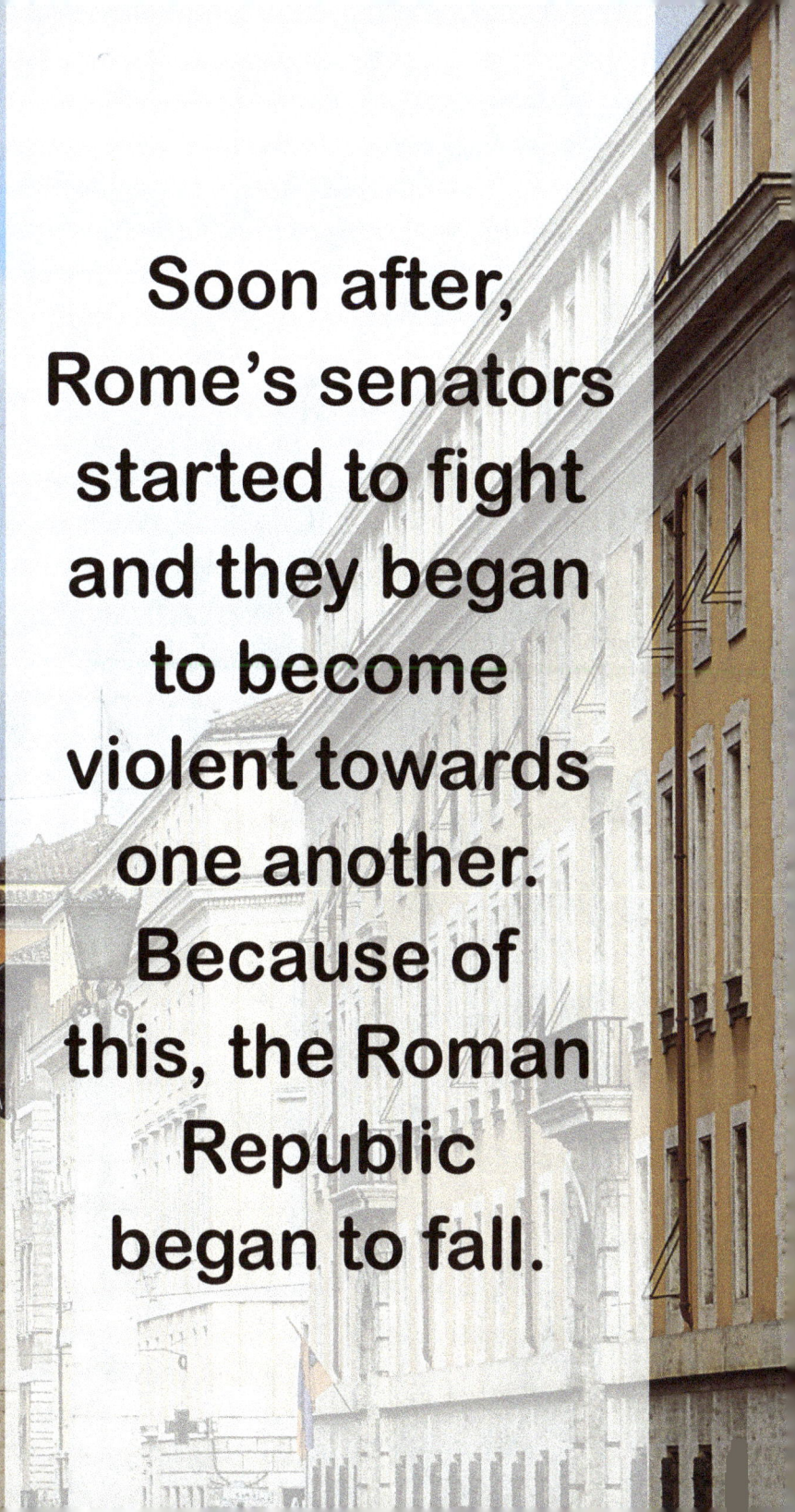

The fall of the Republic began in 59 BC, with the union of the three powerful Roman politicians: Julius Caesar, Pompey the Great, and Marcus Licinius Crassus. They were known as the First Triumvirate.

When Crassus died in 53 BC, Pompey and Caesar became enemies.

In 45 BC, Caesar defeated Pompey and he ruled the Roman Republic as the supreme ruler.

Julius Caesar declared himself the ruler for life, but it didn't last long as he was assassinated a year later.

When Caesar was murdered in 44 B.C., Caesar's nephew, Octavian, became the new leader of Rome.

Octavian introduced the Empire government. He became the first Roman emperor. Octavian later on changed his name to "Augustus".

In the new government, the Emperor had the supreme power although the lower-level government was still in existence.

The first Roman Empire was one of the most prosperous empires as it made Rome very wealthy.

The Roman Empire remained a powerful force for the next 300 years.

There is much more to know about the Ancient Roman government. Did you enjoy learning about the Roman Government? Share this book with your friends!

www.ingramcontent.com/pod-product-compliance
Lightning Source LLC
Chambersburg PA
CBHW081233020426
42331CB00012B/3156

9 781683 765936